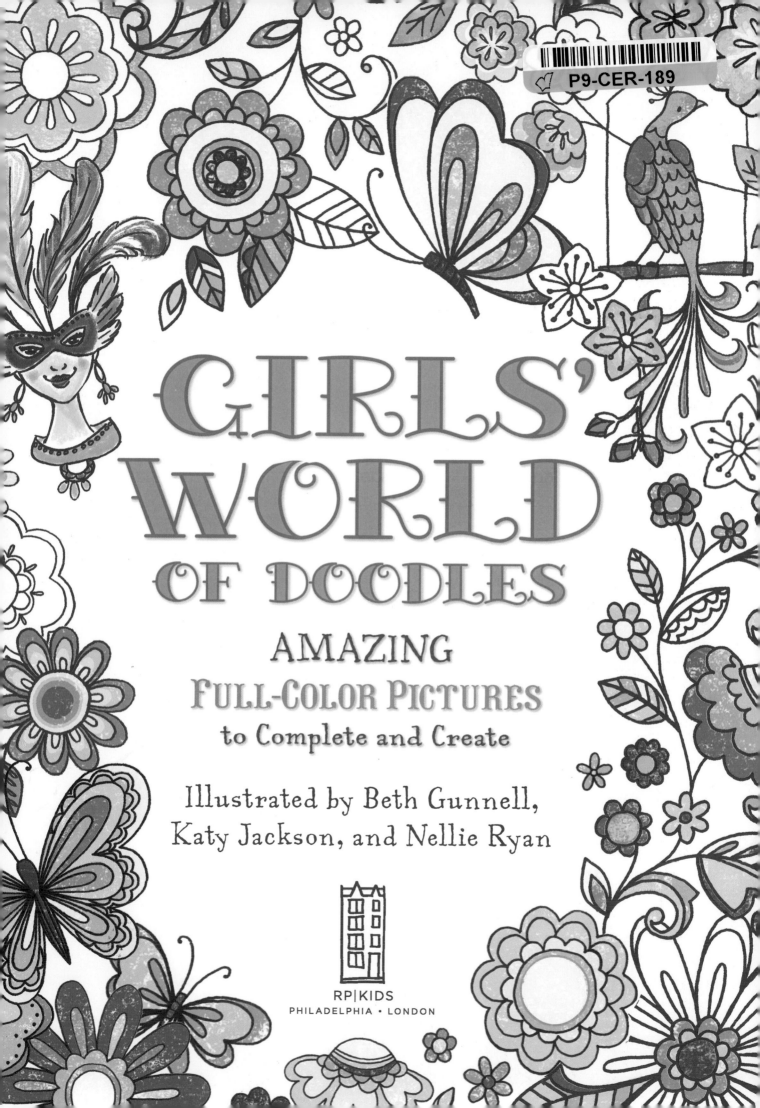

GIRLS' WORLD OF DOODLES

AMAZING
FULL-COLOR PICTURES
to Complete and Create

Illustrated by Beth Gunnell,
Katy Jackson, and Nellie Ryan

RP|KIDS
PHILADELPHIA · LONDON

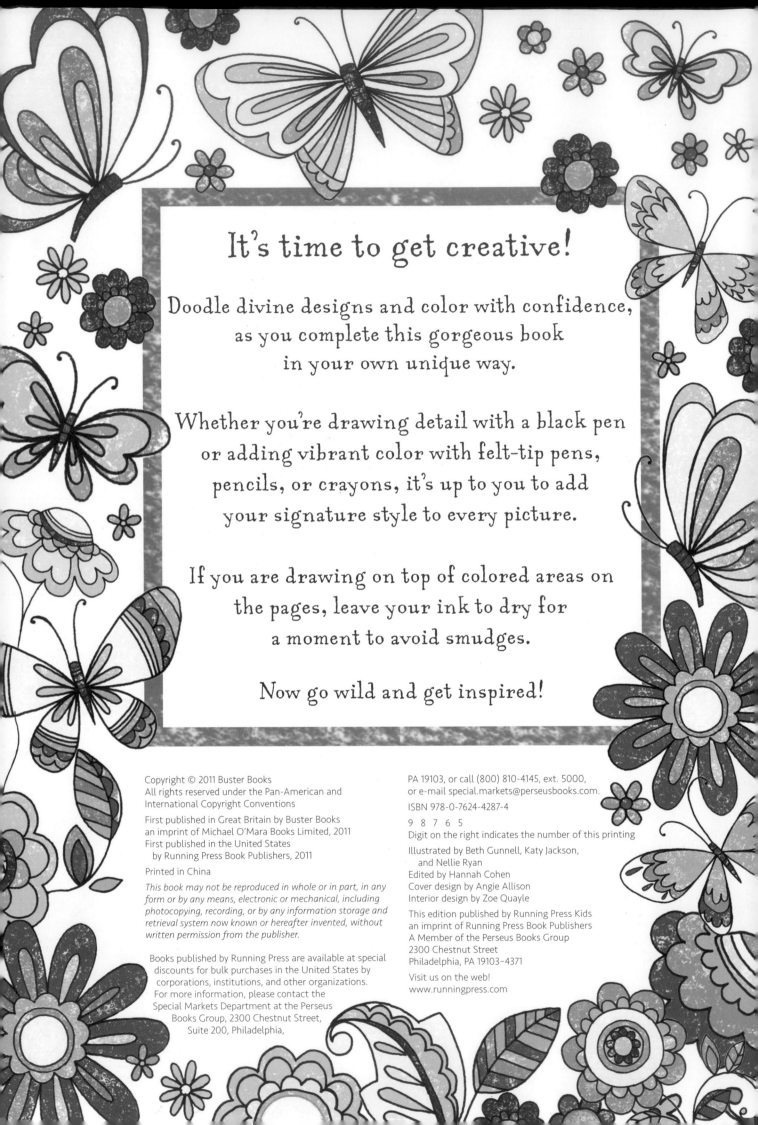

It's time to get creative!

Doodle divine designs and color with confidence,
as you complete this gorgeous book
in your own unique way.

Whether you're drawing detail with a black pen
or adding vibrant color with felt-tip pens,
pencils, or crayons, it's up to you to add
your signature style to every picture.

If you are drawing on top of colored areas on
the pages, leave your ink to dry for
a moment to avoid smudges.

Now go wild and get inspired!

Copyright © 2011 Buster Books
All rights reserved under the Pan-American and
International Copyright Conventions

First published in Great Britain by Buster Books
an imprint of Michael O'Mara Books Limited, 2011
First published in the United States
by Running Press Book Publishers, 2011

Printed in China

This book may not be reproduced in whole or in part, in any
form or by any means, electronic or mechanical, including
photocopying, recording, or by any information storage and
retrieval system now known or hereafter invented, without
written permission from the publisher.

Books published by Running Press are available at special
discounts for bulk purchases in the United States by
corporations, institutions, and other organizations.
For more information, please contact the
Special Markets Department at the Perseus
Books Group, 2300 Chestnut Street,
Suite 200, Philadelphia,

PA 19103, or call (800) 810-4145, ext. 5000,
or e-mail special.markets@perseusbooks.com.

ISBN 978-0-7624-4287-4

9 8 7 6 5
Digit on the right indicates the number of this printing

Illustrated by Beth Gunnell, Katy Jackson,
  and Nellie Ryan
Edited by Hannah Cohen
Cover design by Angie Allison
Interior design by Zoe Quayle

This edition published by Running Press Kids
an imprint of Running Press Book Publishers
A Member of the Perseus Books Group
2300 Chestnut Street
Philadelphia, PA 19103–4371

Visit us on the web!
www.runningpress.com

Add more beautiful birds and bridges.

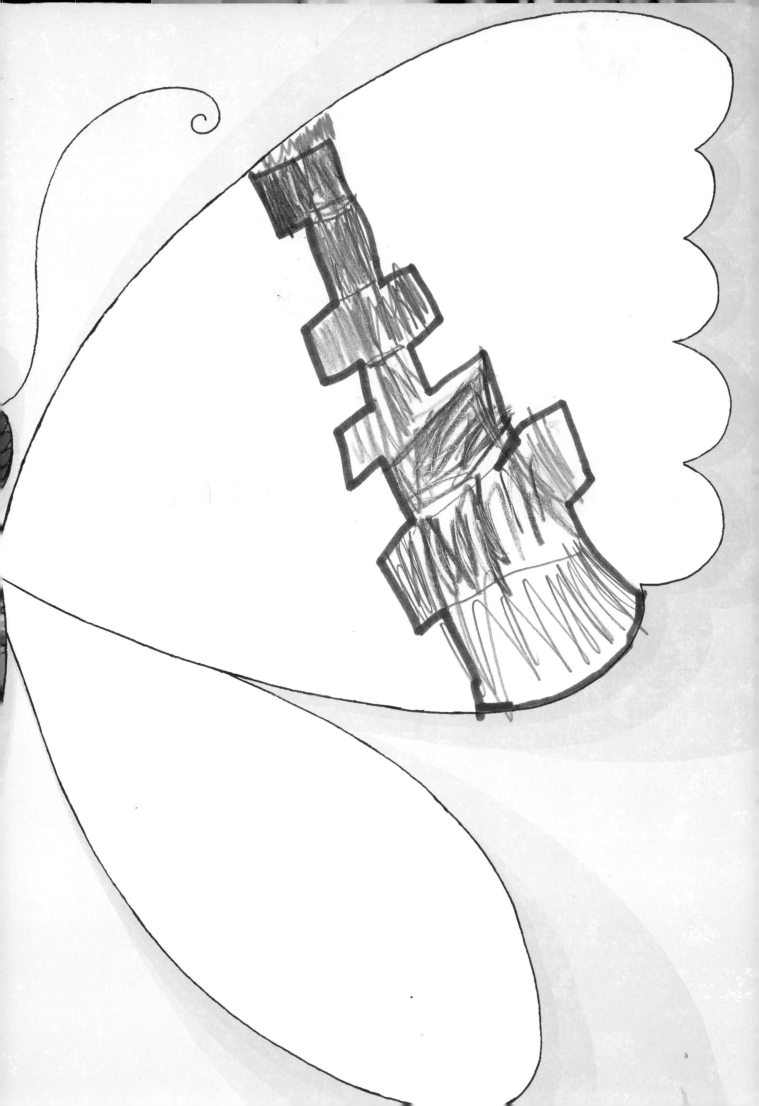

Fill the trees with owls.

Complete and color the floral design.

Decorate the china for afternoon tea.

Complete the gorgeous screen.

Add more fantastic feathers to these carnival masks.

Go fruit and nuts!

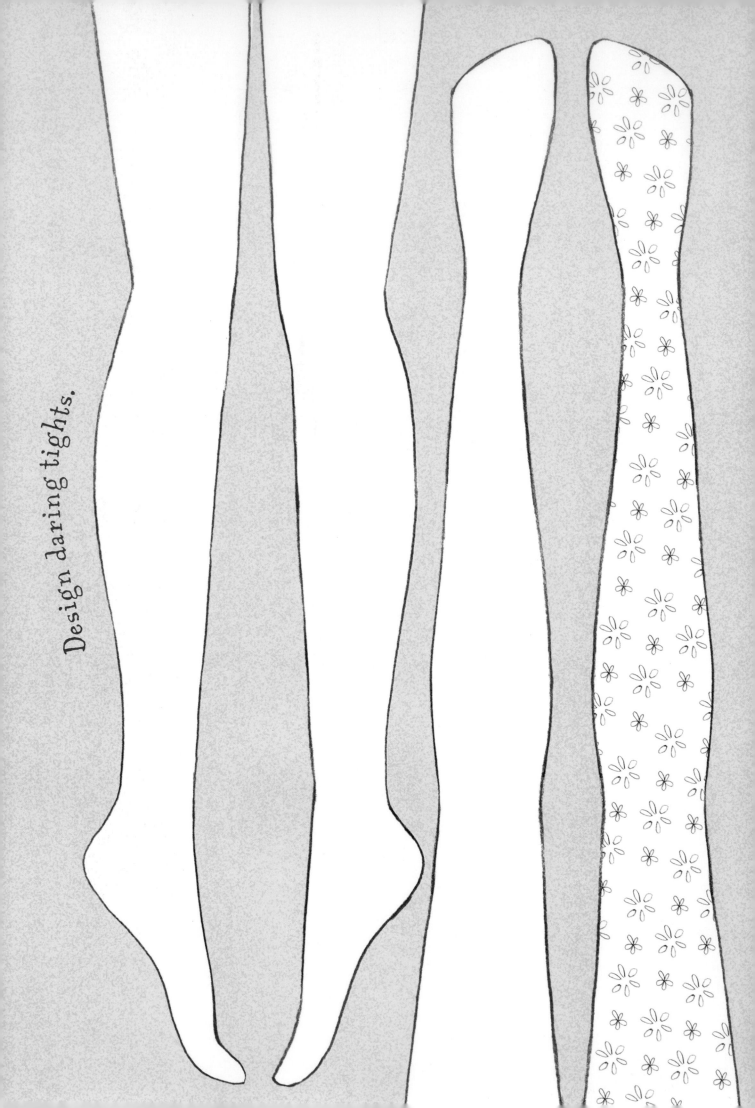

Design daring tights.

Bright, beautiful buttons!

Color in
this classic
pattern.

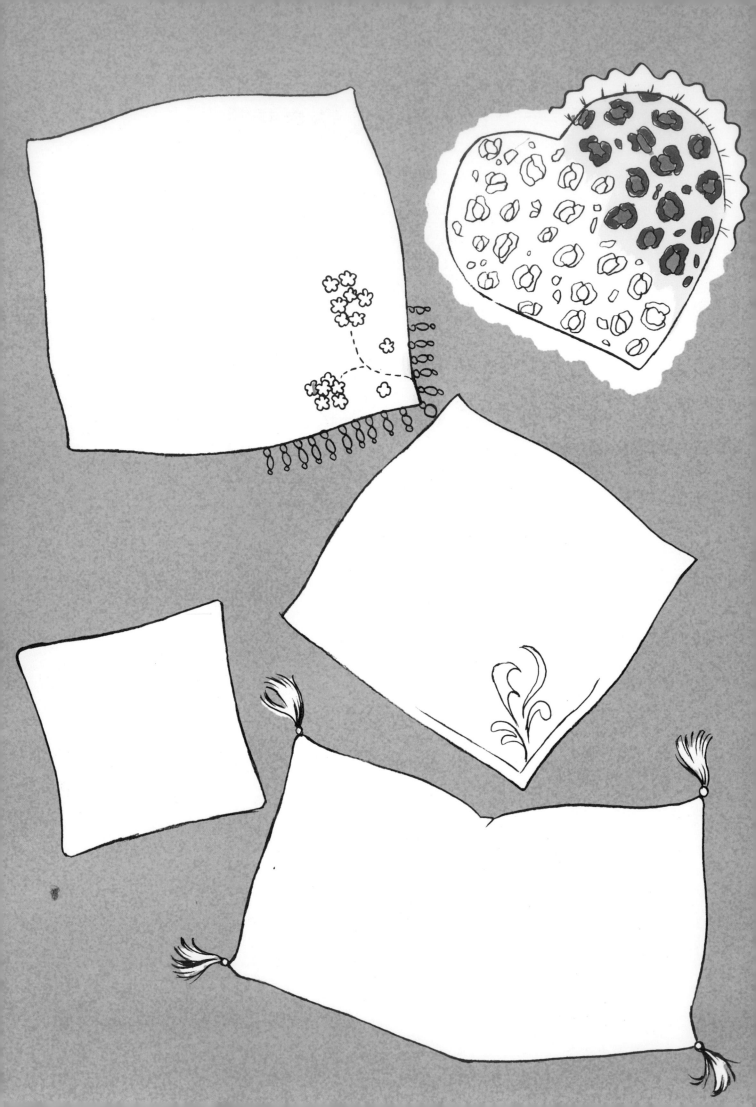

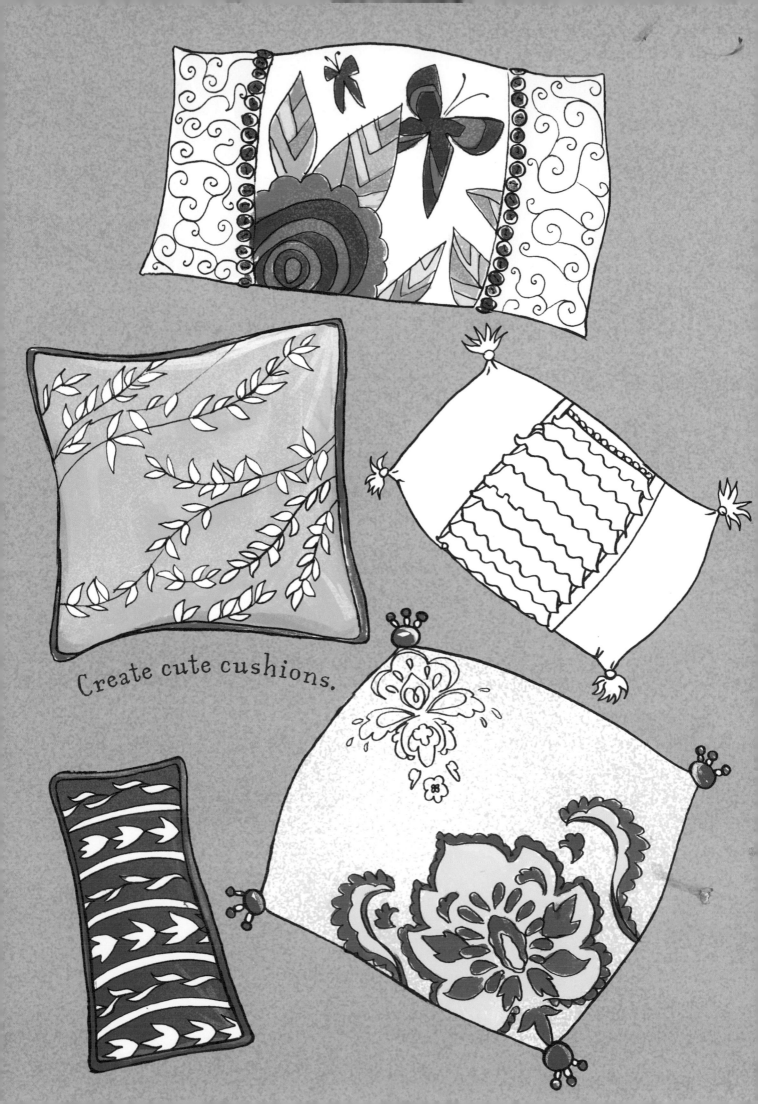

Create cute cushions.

Complete the daisy chain.

Dreamy ice creams . . .

. . . and luscious lollipops.

Decorate the girls' kimonos.

Fill in the flowers.

Create heavenly headscarves and bright bandanas.

Complete the creepy-crawlies.

Fill the photo album with pictures of your friends.

Fill the page with beautiful butterflies.

Colorful kites!

Give these girls
designer swimwear
and trendy towels.

Fill the jars with sweets.

Scatter the shore with seashells.

Finish the stylish leaf-and-petal pattern.

Bold bangles . . .

. . . and bright bracelets.

Fill the page with fans, flowers, and fabulous shapes.

Decorate these Russian dolls.

Create a pretty paisley pattern.

Make this heart burst with beautiful patterns.

Give the peacocks
fantastic feathers.

Decorate the daring designer shoes.

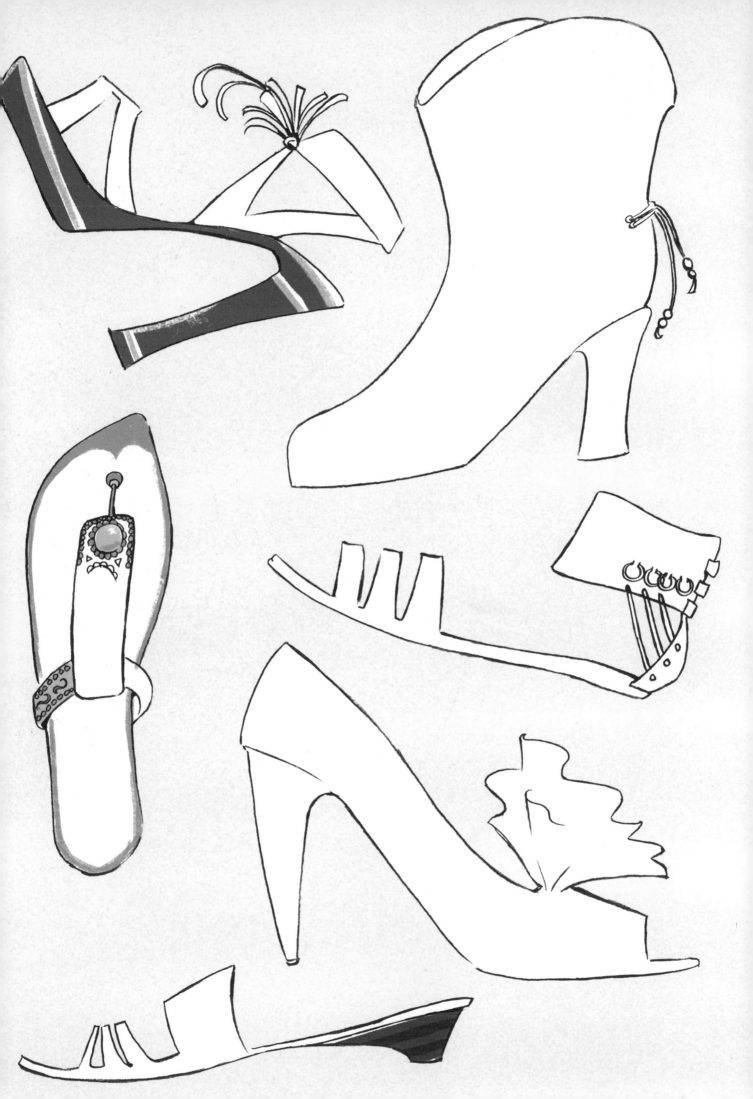

Make the swirl even more stylish.

Beautiful bunting blowing in the breeze.

Add to this design inspired by Aboriginal art.

Decorate the balloons.

Bags of style.

Perfect the pattern.

Finish this stylish sari.

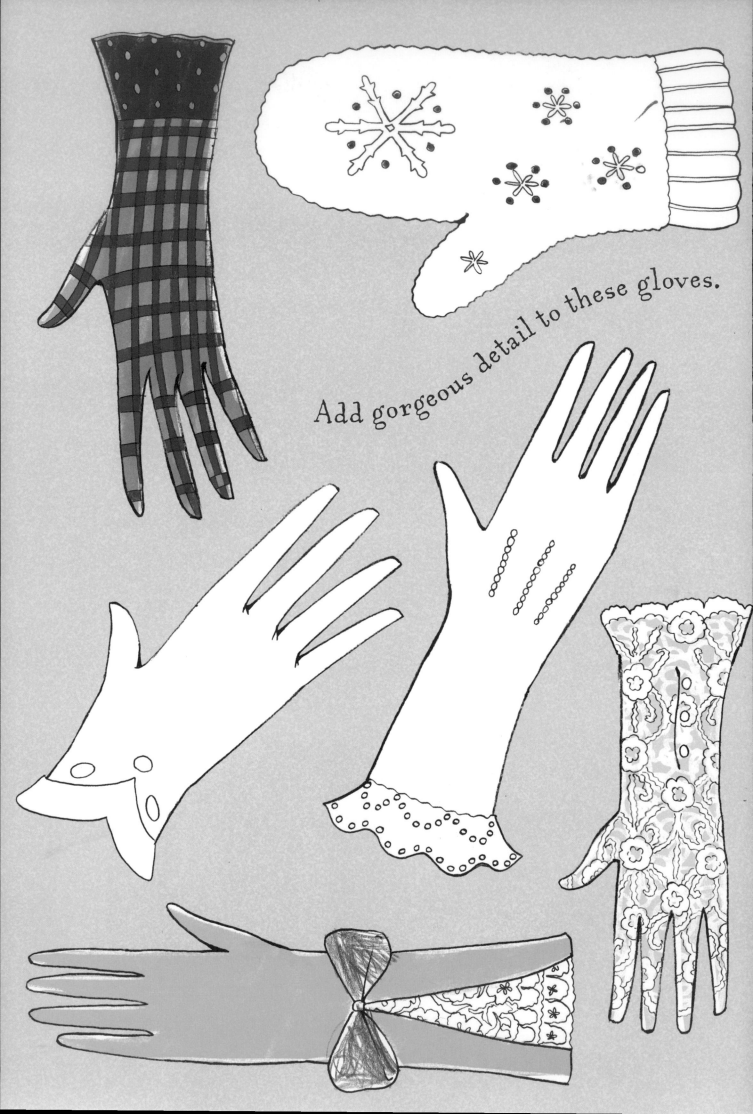

Add gorgeous detail to these gloves.

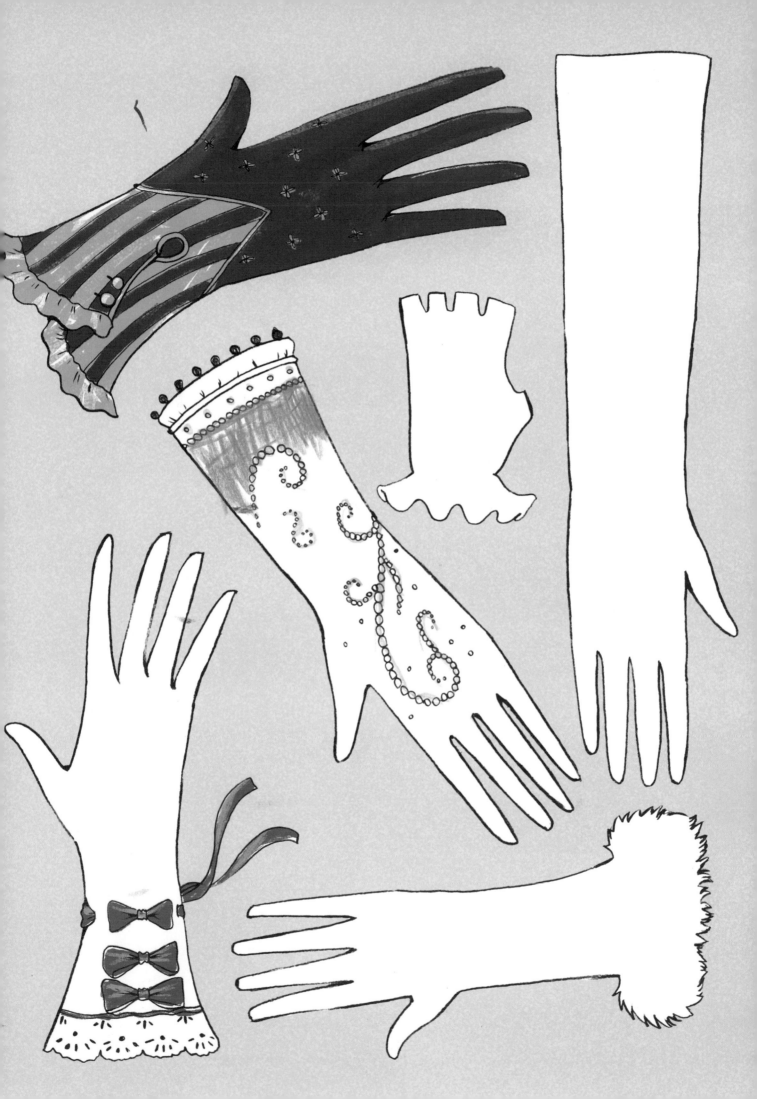

Complete the blushing bride's outfit.

Make these tiaras twinkle.

Create a perfect pool.

Build more towering totem poles.

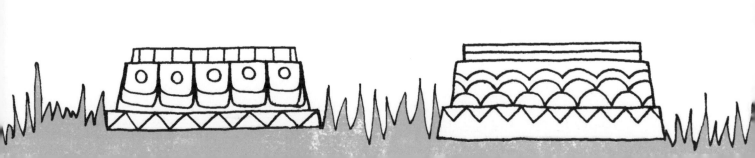

Give the coat, boots, and umbrella a splash of color.

Design vintage umbrellas.

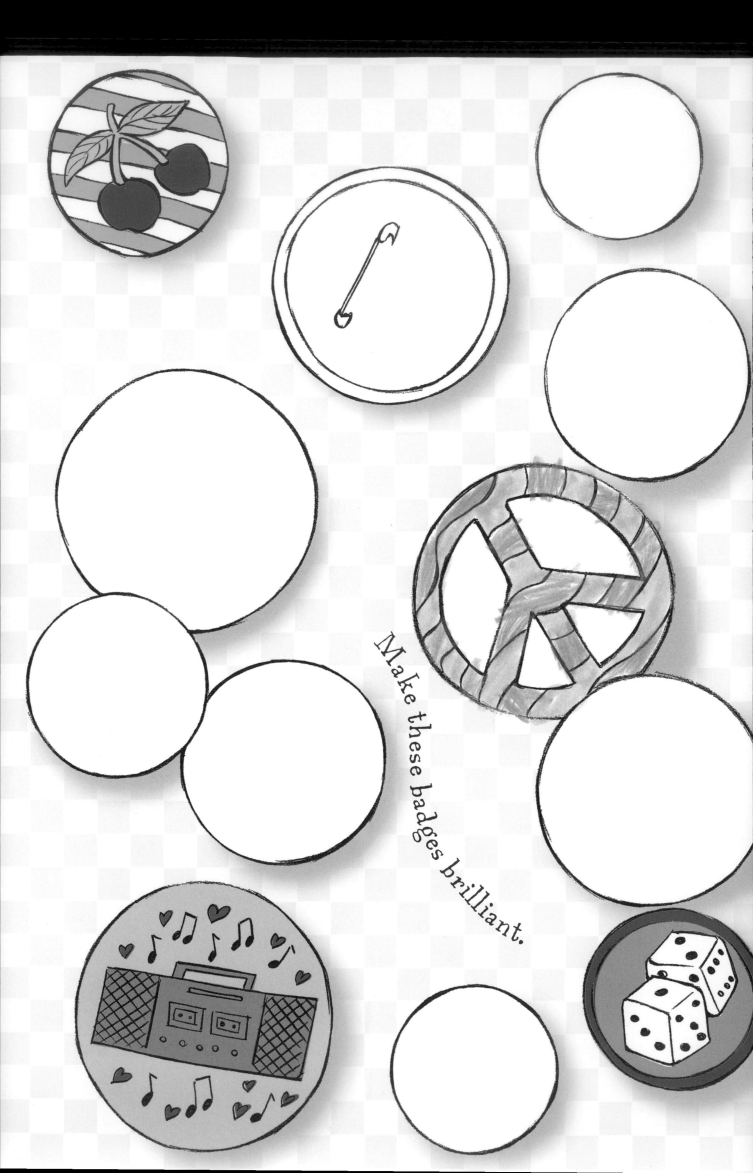

Make these badges brilliant.

Finish the stained-glass window.

Make the backpacks and sneakers pretty.

Design
fantastic
tiles.

Fabulous fruit that's totally tropical!

Design some sassy shades.

Finish these feathery hats.

Hands up for henna!

Art attack!

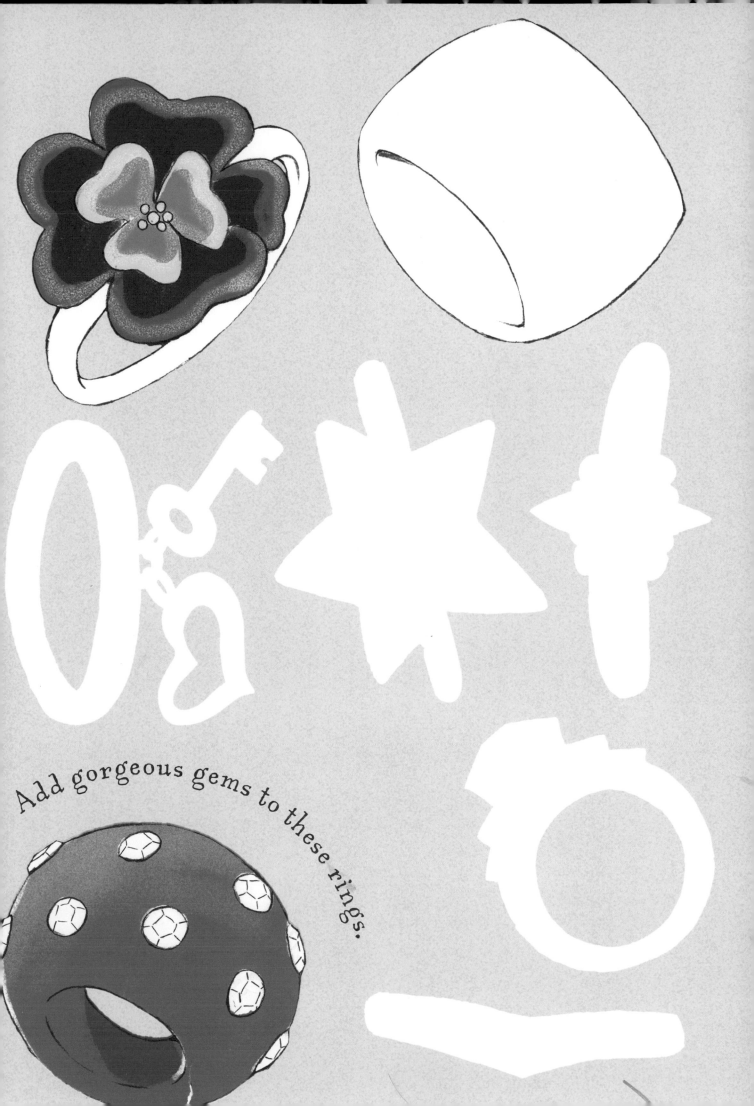

Add gorgeous gems to these rings.

Cook up some colorful cupcakes.

Give these boats sensational sails.

Finish these hair accessories and headbands.

Decorate the page with snowflakes.

Design your own trendy tops.